EDWARD FITZGERALD

LIEUTENANT COLONEL, RTD.

THE BRITISH ARMY

Illustrated by

VICTOR G. AMBRUS

London

OXFORD UNIVERSITY PRESS

1964

Oxford University Press, Amen House, London, E.C.4.

GLASGOW NEW YORK TORONTO MELBOURNE WELLINGTON
BOMBAY CALCUTTA MADRAS KARACHI LAHORE DACCA
CAPE TOWN SALISBURY NAIROBI IBADAN ACCRA
KUALA LUMPUR HONG KONG

FIRST PUBLISHED 1964

*The author gratefully acknowledges
the help given to him by Mr. Ronald Welch.*

Printed in England by Jesse Broad & Co. Ltd. at Old Trafford, Manchester 16

EARLY TIMES

The earliest armed forces of Britain were those who opposed the might of the Roman legions when, fifty-five years before the birth of Christ, they landed on the shores of Britain and invaded and conquered the land.

In the 'Dark Ages', when the Romans had gone, Britain was attacked again and again — by the Vikings, the Northmen, and finally by William the Conqueror. In those days she had no organized army ; men were not trained as soldiers, and unskilled troops were only raised if and when the need arose. When William the Conqueror landed in 1066, Harold's small forces were quickly defeated by the skill of the French archers.

But in medieval times things began to change. A form of National Service came into being ; all fit men were trained to use the bow, and they were all liable to be 'called

The medieval Army on the march

up' in an emergency. An army would be recruited to fight in a particular campaign or expedition. Most of the troops were raised by the local lords or landowners from among the retainers of their estates. The men fought under their own master's standard or banner, and when the campaign was over they would return to the land and their normal peace-time jobs.

The more adventurous among them became soldiers of fortune, and left England to serve in other armies as paid mercenaries. Many foreign mercenaries, usually either German or Dutch, were used by the Kings of England to fight against the French.

In those days battles were usually decided by the cavalry – knights on horseback who wore chain-mail armour and fought with swords and battle-axes. Later on,

The first muskets were heavy, clumsy weapons

however, with the invention of the Long Bow, the foot soldier regained pride of place on the battlefield, for now he could hit the enemy at a far greater distance than before, and prepare the way for a cavalry attack. The English bowmen became feared all over the Continent after their two great victories at Crécy and Agincourt.

By 1558, the firearm had begun to appear on the battlefield in place of the Long Bow. The musket of this time was a clumsy, heavy weapon, which had so much recoil when it was fired that a rest had to be driven into the ground to support it. Body-armour, which was unwieldy, began to disappear. A definite battle-formation started to take shape, too, with the pikemen standing in the centre of the unit, flanked by the musketeers, with the cavalry in the rear and the artillery guns placed in pairs between the units.

All this time — up to the seventeenth century — there was no standing army in England. The country disliked the idea of a standing army, for fear that a dangerous and powerful weapon might be placed in the hands of the King. It is interesting that, from the seventeenth century right up until 1955, an Army Act had to be passed each year to keep the Army legally in being, and to vote a sum of money for its upkeep. Today, for the sake of convenience, the Act is passed only every five years. Although the Army swears allegiance to the Crown, it is still controlled by Parliament.

CROMWELL AND THE NEW MODEL ARMY

The beginnings of a permanent and organized army date from the time of Oliver Cromwell. During the Civil War, the armies of both Charles I and of Parliament were composed of amateur soldiers. Cromwell, however, formed the Parliamentary troops into the first regular force in Britain, the New Model Army. He introduced proper rates of pay and rations; he organized regiments of foot and horse with trained officers and good equipment, and he also introduced the red-coat-uniform which was to remain the colour of the British Army for the next hundred years.

Oliver Cromwell

Royal Horse Guard, c. 1742

The New Model Army as such came to an end in 1647. The present Army as we know it is about 300 years old, and was formed at the time of the Reformation for the personal use of King Charles II. Units were retained both from the Royalist side and from Parliament's New Model Army. These regiments were: The Coldstream Guards, the Life Guards, the Grenadier Guards, and the Royal Horse Guards (The Blues). The Royal Scots, as we know them today, were at that time a French regiment, and became the First of Foot.

At about this time, Tangiers came into Charles's possession through his Queen's dowry, and the Queen's Royal Surrey Regiment and the Royal Dragoons were raised for service there — the first regiments to be stationed abroad. Afterwards other regiments were gradually added to the Army, and were usually called after the name of their Colonel.

The first great war in which the Army fought was against the French in the War of the Grand Alliance, 1688-97, when it served in Flanders under William III.

THE GREAT DAYS OF MARLBOROUGH

In 1702, when the Army was once again at war, the Commander-in-Chief was John Churchill, Duke of Marlborough, a direct ancestor of Sir Winston Churchill. The Duke was undoubtedly the most brilliant of all British generals, and his battles and those of the next 200 years cannot be easily understood without a description of the arms used by the soldiers of those times, or the tactics used on the battlefield.

The Duke of Marlborough

The chief weapon was the flintlock musket, which changed but little during the next 150 years. Powder and bullet were loaded separately by being rammed down the long barrel from the muzzle end ; this naturally had to be done standing up, in full view of the enemy. Specially fine powder was then poured into the priming pan ; when the trigger was pressed, the flint flew forward, hit a piece of metal called the frizzen, and the sparks ignited the priming powder. The flash passed through a small vent hole into the breech of the musket, and exploded the main charge.

All this, of course, took a long time and the foot soldier was given a bayonet as protection whilst he was reloading to the accompaniment of many shouted orders. The musket, 'Brown Bess', or the 'Tower Musket' as it was called, had a smooth barrel, and the bullet came out without spinning in any way. Even a faint breeze would deflect it to one side or the other, and only a lucky shot would hit a target at over two hundred

Loading the 'Brown Bess' musket

Infantry in action

yards. The gunpowder gave off a dense white smoke, and the battlefields of those days were soon covered with a thick grey fog.

The slow rate of fire, two rounds a minute, perhaps, and no more, meant that troops fought in close formation. Large armies manoeuvred on quite small pieces of ground, and but for the drifting smoke of the gunfire, a general could quite easily see everything that was happening to his army. Infantry advanced against each other shoulder-to-shoulder in column or line, halted, and then exchanged volleys at point-blank range, firing rank by rank or even regiment by regiment, every man loading to the shouted words of command, every ramrod going down together, every pan primed at the same moment, and hundreds of muskets coming up to the aim. Then came the single shattering roar of the explosions, the rolling bank of smoke, and once more the shouts of the officers, the precise, jerky drill of reloading, all this at a murderously short range, until one side broke and retreated, leaving behind long lines of dead and wounded.

The British uniforms of Marlborough's Army were a mass of bright colours, for concealment was unnecessary on the small and crowded battlefields of his time. The

A Highlander, a 'Royal Regiment' Sergeant and an Artillery officer in Marlborough's Army

cavalry wore three-cornered hats, red coats, white breeches and long black riding boots. They were armed with swords, pistols, or muskets, for the British cavalry was trained by Marlborough to fight both on horseback and on foot. The infantry wore much longer red coats, white breeches and gaiters, and black shoes. Grenadiers wore tall mitre-shaped hats ; one of these hats can be seen now in the National Army Museum at Sandhurst. Besides their heavy musket and bayonet, they carried a large knapsack, and cross belts holding bullets and powder.

The French Army against which the British fought had the reputation of being the most successful in Europe, and it was thought that there was no general to equal the famous French Marshals in brilliance and experience. In 1704 Marlborough marched his army from Holland into the heart of Germany, for the French were threatening to capture Vienna, the capital of the Austrians, Britain's allies. Such a long march so far from one's base was exceptionally difficult in the eighteenth century ; the roads were dreadful even in summer, and slow horse transport was the only method of sending supplies of food, ammunition and equipment.

But Marlborough's march to the Danube was a masterpiece of planning and organization. Everything had been foreseen; some of the supplies came by river barges and at every stage the Army found all they needed, even new boots and clothing, and they arrived in Germany intact and with a very high morale. If Marlborough's reputation depended upon that march alone, he would still rank high among the great generals of the world. The battle of Blenheim that followed was the first great victory

won by the British, and also one of the most decisive and brilliant in the long history of the Army. Before the war ended in 1714, Marlborough had won two more outstanding battles, those of Ramillies and Oudenarde. It was no wonder that his greatness as a soldier was recognized by every nation in Europe at the time. The French had good reason to fear him, and his name became familiar in France through the tune of the famous song, 'Marlbrook s'en va-t-en guerre', the tune that we sing to the chorus of 'He's a jolly good fellow'.

There was, indeed, only one Marlborough. After the end of the Marlborough campaigns the Army was drastically cut down to the tiny figure of 12,000 (though this was raised twenty years later to about 18,000). But even during the Seven Years' War in the middle of the century the total was only just over 60,000. The country was still reluctant to allow a large army, and even the most modest demands for money were opposed by Parliament.

The march to the Danube

Living conditions for the men in the ranks were appalling. There were no barracks, and troops were scattered all over the countryside in squalid inns. The pay of an infantry private, by the time he had paid various deductions, was whittled down from 3*s*. 6*d*. to 6*d*. a week, and his slightest crime was punished by ferocious flogging. Recruits, as might be expected, came from the unemployable, the scum of the country, and it is surprising that on the battlefield the British soldier still showed the same courage and stolid determination that had made Marlborough's Army so famous.

VICTORIES OF THE EIGHTEENTH CENTURY

In 1743 Britain was once more at war with France, and at Dettingen George II was the last British monarch to lead his troops into battle.

The next great war was the Seven Years' War, from 1756-63, in which Britain fought with Prussia against the French. Unlike the usual campaigns in Europe, this was mainly a struggle for supremacy between the French and the British in India and North America, both countries trying to gain more colonies.

In 1757, in India, Clive defeated a native army of 50,000 at Plassey, though his own force numbered only 3,000. He had one regular British battalion with him, the Dorsetshires, who later inscribed the words 'Primus in Indis' on their cap-badges to show that they were the first regiment to serve in India.

The year 1758 was for Britain a year of continued success. Pitt's genius as a war minister was everywhere beginning to be felt, and one of the factors contributing to his success was his ability to pick good commanders in the field, and to employ them regardless of their age or seniority.

Part of Pitt's plan was to strike a blow at the heart of French Canada, and the capture of Louisburg made possible an advance up the Saint Lawrence River to attack Quebec. Quebec was the main stronghold of the French in Canada, and to capture it would be

The war in India

a tremendous British victory. For this task he selected an outstanding young brigadier of thirty-one, named James Wolfe, and gave him the temporary rank of Major-General. Wolfe was commissioned at the age of fifteen ; he was an adjutant at the battle of Dettingen a year later, and was now a veteran of many campaigns. He was also a student in the art of war, an unusual thing for an officer of his day. It was his planning and tactics that had brought about the surrender of Louisburg, but, unfortunately, his health was failing and from time to time he suffered from bouts of fever and acute pain. His doctor managed to keep him on his feet for this, his greatest, and what turned out to be his final campaign.

The strong fortress of Quebec is situated on a rocky hill which overhangs the river St. Lawrence. Just beyond Quebec is the high ground known as The Heights of Abraham. This vantage-point was commanded by the French under their very able general, Montcalm, and the steep crags of the cliffs were in themselves almost impenetrable and safe from any form of attack.

Up to this time, Montcalm had been causing great embarrassment to the British by his brilliant defensive tactics. Wolfe's forces numbered only about half those of the French, and time was running short, for the St. Lawrence River would soon be ice-bound. Nevertheless, Wolfe's expedition set sail under Admiral Saunders through the dangerous course of the narrow river, and eventually a possible landing-place was found some

The attack on Quebec

two miles west of the city. After much searching, Wolfe found a zig-zag track leading up the cliffs. On the evening of 12th September, the main body of assault troops, about 1,600 strong, was rowed silently to their landing-place and put ashore. The boatcrews used muffled oars and no lights, a fine piece of navigation and seamanship.

Throughout the night the troops continued their Herculean task of scaling the cliffs, under cover of a tremendous bombardment by Saunders' fleet as a decoy. By first light, Wolfe and his men had formed up in battle formation face to face with the French lines, and the French were taken completely by surprise. Wolfe gave the order to charge and the exultant British lines surged forward with the bayonet, causing a shattering defeat for the French. The battle which followed found them in utter confusion, the ground littered with their dead and wounded. A few days later Quebec surrendered, and French supremacy in Canada came to an end.

Both Wolfe and Montcalm were mortally wounded during the battle, but Wolfe lived to see his men in their finest moments of victory, and died knowing that the fate of Quebec was settled. This had been a fine victory for Britain, but also a great loss to the country of such an outstanding young general. It is not surprising to know that the memory of Wolfe is kept alive in many regiments of the Army today.

Meanwhile, in Europe, another British Army had joined forces with its German allies, and in 1759, the same year as Quebec, it met the French at the battle of Minden in Germany. It was here that a brigade of British infantry, through a mistake in orders, advanced against the massed lines of the French cavalry, 10,000 strong, a manoeuvre that would normally have been suicidal. As they marched off, the six Minden regiments picked roses in the gardens through which they passed, and stuck them in their hats. They then came under a heavy cross-fire of guns, but they marched steadily on in their thin line formation, heading for the French cavalry. Three times in all the French hurled themselves at their opponents, but on each occasion, to the astonishment of the French, the British proceeded to dress their

Before the battle of Minden

depleted ranks as if they were on the parade ground. Up came their muskets, and the scene was blotted out by the cloud of white smoke. Down went the front ranks of the cavalry. Eventually all seventy-five squadrons of cavalry were pushed off the field in disorder: a magnificent victory for the British. The Minden regiments were: The Lancashire Fusiliers, The Royal Welch Fusiliers, The King's Own Scottish Borderers, The Royal Hampshire Regiment, The King's Own Yorkshire Light Infantry, and The Suffolk Regiment. On the 1st August each year these regiments, with the exception of the Royal Welch Fusiliers, parade with roses in their caps in memory of that wonderful feat. Whatever may have been the conditions under which the British soldier of the eighteenth century existed, he was still, on the battlefield, the steadiest and most determined soldier in Europe.

In peace-time the Army was once more cut down and little was done to improve the conditions of the soldiers. One of the most extraordinary customs was the practice by which anyone with sufficient money could buy himself a commission as an officer. In fact, he could go on buying his promotion up to the rank of Colonel without any question of his age, his experience or his knowledge of warfare.

In 1790, for instance, Colonels of regiments were asked how many of their Captains were under the age of 12, and how many Lieutenant-Colonels were under 18. The Duke of Wellington bought his way up to the command of a regiment before he had seen any active service. There was a regular scale of prices laid down, but these were usually ignored, and there was a 'Black Market' price.

Some improvements, however, did take place. At Marlborough's suggestion, the Artillery was placed on a permanent footing. The Royal Regiment of Artillery came into existence, and in 1741 Woolwich Academy was founded to train the gunner officers. The one great advantage of the Artillery was that promotion depended entirely upon seniority and merit — not on purchase. So good was their training and so effective their guns that the regiment soon became one of the finest artillery corps in the world.

Gunners training at Woolwich Academy

American Irregulars

TIMES OF CHANGE

In 1775, one of the most unfortunate occurrences in the long history of the British Army took place. This was the American War of Independence, when the Army had to go to war against some of its own colonies. At the time there was a complete lack of understanding between Westminster and the colonies. The Government at Westminster soon found that mobilizing for a war that was to be fought 3,000 miles away from home was a formidable task; public opinion was divided and there was a general lack of enthusiasm for the American War.

The American troops were commanded by General George Washington, whose skilful handling of an Army inferior in numbers, equipment, and discipline completely outmanoeuvred the British leaders on many occasions. The British troops fought magnificently throughout the war, despite the indifference of the Government, the difficulties of terrain, physical hardships and sickness. But their equipment was clumsy, and in their bright red coats the British soldiers were unsuitably clad for guerilla warfare, where full use is made of the smallest fold in the ground, or the cover afforded by rocks and trees. Here was a case when a well-led irregular Army who knew their country defeated superior forces.

In 1801 General Abercromby defeated the French Army in Egypt at the battle of Alexandria, where the Gloucestershire Regiment was attacked by the French Grenadiers in front and in the rear. The rear rank of the Gloucesters turned about, and beat off both attacks. In recognition of this, the regiment was allowed to wear a badge on the back of their head-dress, and later they also adopted a small badge of the Sphinx, in memory of Egypt.

Uniforms were changing again, and were now more suited for the battlefield. The detested queue (hair worn in plaits) was abolished in 1808. One regiment, however, the Royal Welch Fusiliers, was overseas when the order was issued, and when they arrived in England they were still wearing their queues, the last regiment to be doing so. To commemorate this, all officers and men of the regiment are today allowed to wear a small black strip of silk on the back of their collars.

The uncomfortable gaiters went too, and were replaced by blue-grey trousers. The head-dress changed to a black shako shaped like a stove pipe, and one of these can be seen in the National Army Museum, together with the bullet hole that nearly killed its owner at Waterloo. The tunic was still red, but became much shorter.

As a result of the campaigns in the North American forests, where the red coat was far too conspicuous, several special regiments were formed, including the Rifle Brigade, who were given a dark-green uniform. This need for camouflage became even more apparent when the new Baker Rifle appeared. Although it took just as long to reload as the old Tower Musket, for the bullet fitted the barrel much more tightly, the Baker Rifle had a longer range and was far more accurate than the old Tower Musket; it could therefore be fired from a greater — and safer — distance. At this time, too, some Light Infantry Regiments were formed, trained to move in a more open formation than the formal masses of the eighteenth century. The pattern of warfare was changing.

The Rifle Brigade with the new Baker Rifle

In 1808, Napoleon, at the height of his power, invaded Spain, and a British force was sent to the help of the Spanish, under the command of Sir John Moore. Moore was not only a charming and fascinating personality, but also one of the greatest trainers of soldiers in the history of the Army. The fine quality of his regiments was soon recognized, and earned the nickname of 'the Brigade'.

Moore's force had reached a place called Sahagun when a rumour went round that the Emperor Napoleon was advancing with a powerful Army. The Spanish troops decided to retreat all along the line, and Moore was also compelled to retreat towards the sea with his small force. The retreat was carried out with great suffering and loss, but eventually the British force reached the town of Corunna in the north-west corner of Spain. A fleet of British warships was expected at Corunna, but the speed of the

The death of General Moore

pursuing enemy threatened to destroy the whole British force before the warships arrived. Moore therefore ordered his men to stand their ground and fight. The battle that followed enabled the British forces to reach the ships in safety, but unfortunately the gallant general was killed in action.

Moore was succeeded by the Duke of Wellington who had already fought in India. There he had learned the vital importance of transport and supply, and it is typical of him that one of his written orders in Spain dealt with the question of bullock waggons. A somewhat aloof man with a wonderfully clear and concise brain, Wellington ranks second only to Marlborough as a great British commander.

It is difficult to pick out any particular battle from the Peninsular War, or to mention any special regiment, for Wellington's Army (together with Marlborough's Army and the British Expeditionary Force of 1914) is one of the three greatest British Armies. Wellington fought a series of campaigns in Spain, inflicting 200,000 casualties upon the

The Duke of Wellington

French, winning twenty battles, capturing four great fortresses and finishing by driving the French over the Pyrenees and invading France itself. Still today, some of the proudest battle honours on regimental colours are those of the Peninsula, and such names as Corunna, Busaco, Talavera, Albuera, Badajoz and Salamanca ring out like trumpet calls. They are, all of them, magnificent and inspiring stories that must be read in detail.

Napoleon abdicated in 1814 and was sent to exile on Elba, but he escaped and returned to France in a last effort to regain his throne. He was beaten, however, by an allied force of British and Prussians at Waterloo in 1815. Wellington, the only general who had consistently defeated the French Marshals, commanded the British troops, but he had a poorly trained Army, and few of his Peninsular veterans.

Wellington fought a defensive battle all day on the ridge outside Waterloo, waiting for the Prussians to join him. Early in the battle Napoleon sent forward a huge mass of infantry in column. Lord Uxbridge, the commander of the British cavalry, immediately attacked with the Life Guards, The Blues, and the First Dragoon Guards, and the Union Brigade of the Royals, the Scots Greys and the Inniskilling Dragoons. They swept aside the armoured horsemen and crashed at full gallop into the French infantry columns with such weight and speed that the next morning the French muskets were to be seen lying on the ground in long lines where their owners had laid them down in surrender. As the Scots Greys passed through the British infantry, a Highland regiment leapt up, and catching hold of the Scots Greys' stirrups, charged with them.

At the end of the day, and when the Prussians were beginning to arrive and press on his right wing, Napoleon threw in his last and finest troops, the infantry of the Imperial Guard, tall moustached veterans who had marched into most of the capitals of Europe,

The battle of Waterloo: a cavalry attack

and who had never yet been driven back. In their usual column formation, with their officers urging them on with waving swords and shakos, the drummers pounding away at the *Pas de Charge* with its blood-stirring rhythm of 'Rumadum, dummadum, dum !' the Guards emerged from the smoke and tramped majestically up the hill, heading for the centre of the British position.

But Wellington, as cool and clear-headed as ever, was ready for them and had drawn up his infantry in line formation, two deep, so as to give every man an opportunity to fire. Not a formation for unsteady troops, but these were the Grenadier Guards, and on their flank was one of the Peninsular regiments, the 52nd (now the 1st Green Jackets).

As the bearskins of the French Guards loomed through the drifting smoke, they met with a frightful volley from the Grenadiers. The French Guards faltered for the first time in their history, and at this critical moment the most experienced regiment under Wellington's command decided the issue. This was the 52nd, one of the famous Light Brigade, and commanded by John Colborne, probably the best regimental officer of his day, and later a Field Marshal. Without waiting for orders, he led the 52nd forward in line, deployed them against the unprotected flank of the Imperial Guard, and ordered them to fire. At that range, and from such veteran soldiers, there could be only one result. Then the Grenadiers and the 52nd went in with the bayonet, and down the slope went the struggling columns of the French.

The rest of the French Army had been watching this great struggle, and saw what they had never seen before. Up went the cry, 'The Guard retreats', and the whole of Napoleon's line broke and fled.

A military prison yard, c. 1835

CONDITIONS IN PEACE-TIME

From 1815 to 1854 there was no major war in Europe, though the British Army fought several campaigns in India. At home there was no change in peace-time conditions, and the attitude of Parliament and the country was still the same, so that as little money as possible was spent on the Army.

There were barracks by this time, but they were bleak, uncomfortable and unhealthy places. The food was poor and monotonous : one pound of bread and three-quarters of a pound of meat a day, and the meat was always boiled beef, with but two meals a day.

A private's pay was 7*s.* 6*d.* a week, but half was taken for rations, and some more for other expenses, leaving him just over 2*d.* a day for himself. He was still flogged mercilessly, and some figures illustrate the results of all this neglect. The rate of death per thousand people in civilian life was between seven and nine ; in the Army it was eighteen per thousand. On tropical stations, such as Jamaica, the figure was 121, and it is said that few soldiers lived for more than ten years in India. The absurd purchase-system for officers still continued, and few of them made any study of their profession.

The Tower Musket had finally disappeared by now, and had been replaced by the Minié Rifle. This was, unfortunately, also a muzzle-loader, but it was fired by a percussion cap instead of a flint, with the ball and charge together in one paper container, so that loading was faster. This container had to be bitten so hard that the charge was exposed to the flash of the cap, and it was greased to keep the powder dry. In India the sepoys thought that the grease was made from pig or cow fat, and as certain Indians consider the pig unclean and the cow sacred, they refused to touch the new ammunition. This was one of the causes of the Indian mutiny.

Altogether the administrative system was chaotic, and such was the state of the Army in 1853 when it was called upon to go to war against the Russians in the Crimea. Yet, in spite of such neglect, the fighting spirit of the British Army emerged again and again.

THE CRIMEAN WAR

At the battle of Balaclava, the Russians made a surprise attack on the British line of supply, such as it was, and pushed forward towards the little port of Balaclava. Their way was barred by the Argyll and Sutherland Highlanders, who were drawn up in two lines, the famous 'thin red line'. The Highlanders halted the Russian horse with one volley; the Argylls coolly swung round to the flank as the Russians changed direction and fired again. The enemy fell back in bewilderment.

The rest of the huge mass of Russian cavalry moved across the front of the Heavy Brigade of British horse, the Royals, the Greys, the Inniskillings, and the 4th and 5th Dragoon Guards, commanded by General Scarlett. General Scarlett had never been on a battlefield before, but he was not only a delightful character and a brave man; he was an intelligent one too. He waited now impatiently while the cavalry were carefully aligned as if on the parade ground and ordered his trumpeter to sound the charge. This time the Russians flooded back in disorder across the front of the Light Cavalry Brigade, the 4th, 8th and 11th Hussars, the 13th Light Dragoons, and the 17th Lancers, all under the command of Lord Cardigan. Despite appeals from his officers, Cardigan refused to charge the disorganized Russian cavalry, as he said he had received no orders

The siege of Sebastopol

to move. Meanwhile the Russians captured some guns and were carrying them away when the order arrived for the Light Brigade to attack. Eventually Cardigan led the Light Brigade forward — in the wrong direction — though the fault was not wholly his. The order was very vague and the higher commanders' intentions were not clear. So the Light Brigade rode unflinchingly into a cauldron of gunfire from all sides, closing the dreadful gaps in their ranks, and charged the guns at the end of the valley down which they rode. Cardigan led them all the way, for whatever his faults he was no coward.

As an example of sheer heroism and unhesitating obedience to orders, the charge is one of the most glorious in the history of the Army, but it was also one of the most futile wastes of men's lives.

Then winter came to the Crimea, and the supply system of the British broke down completely. To the horrors of cold and starvation were added the greater nightmares of the hospital arrangements. Britain, the greatest sea power in the world, with a huge merchant fleet and the most up-to-date factory and industrial system, should have had no difficulty in supplying her Army. But the port of Balaclava was too small, and the only road leading from it became impassable.

The Commissariat responsible for handling and distributing all supplies were tied by regulations and the many forms that had to be completed, and were overwhelmed by the emergency. Even when they had the necessary stores, or knew where they were, which was not often, they could not see the vital need for abandoning their beloved forms. One Colonel came down to the port to beg for stoves for his men who were

Florence Nightingale

dying of disease and cold. The stoves were there, but the Colonel was without the properly signed form. So he went away without the stoves that would have saved some lives that night. Another officer went to buy a handful of nails for his hut; but nails, he was told, were sold only by the ton. So he bought a ton.

In Spain a commissary officer had complained once to Wellington that a certain general threatened to hang him if he did not produce some supplies. 'The General,' the Duke said, 'is a man of his word.' The supplies were produced. But there was no Wellington in the Crimea, and the Army died of cold, semi-starvation, and disease. There were few of the original men left alive when Sebastopol fell in the next spring.

It was clear that drastic reforms for the Army were needed, and the country knew it too, for a report by a correspondent of *The Times* newspaper, the first newspaper to send a correspondent to report on a war, drew attention to the totally inadequate medical facilities on the Crimean battlefield. This report led to the appointment of Florence Nightingale to establish a nursing service in Scutari on the shores of the Bosporus. Her appointment caused quite a stir at the time, as it was unheard-of for a woman to pioneer something like this, and carry it through successfully. Florence Nightingale and her party were the nucleus of the present-day Queen Alexandra's Royal Army Nursing Corps. At one time the 'Q.A.'s', as they are affectionately known, wore a grey cloak and bonnet, with long skirts trailing the ground; for warmer climates, such as those encountered during the Boer War, a rather becoming straw 'boater' was worn, with a scarlet band, and a scarlet-lined parasol was carried. The colours of grey and scarlet have always been retained in the nurses' uniform.

The Army are proud of their nurses, who have served them with devotion and courage in every theatre of war, and who carry on a tradition of distinguished service to the Army dating back to that wonderful 'lady of the lamp', Florence Nightingale.

Up to the time of the Crimean War, wives used to accompany their husbands on active service. In those days there were no married quarters and it was quite a common thing to find a family living in a corner of the barrack-room, partitioned off from the soldiers by a canvas screen. In the day-time the women did the family chores and at night the boys of the family would pop into the beds of the soldiers on guard, while the girls of the family retired behind the parental screen. The life of a soldier's wife was rough, tough, and exciting, and the families were very much part of a regiment.

After the Crimean War, reforms came slowly. In 1868 Cardwell became Secretary of State for War, and the purchase-system for officers went at last. So, too, did flogging in peace-time (but on active service not until 1880). Parade-ground uniforms, far too tight and uncomfortable for war, disappeared also. Soldiers were no longer enlisted for life, but for six years with their regiment and six years in the reserve.

The Army was now rearmed with the Martini-Henry rifle, loaded from the breech instead of the muzzle. This was a change that was to revolutionize the whole tactics of warfare, for now, as it was no longer necessary to stand in the open in full view of the enemy, loading could be carried out quickly and from behind cover. The old numbered infantry regiments were given the names of counties or other titles, with depots in different parts of the country, so that they could recruit locally, and create local patriotic feeling. The general effect of all this was to increase the size and efficiency of the peace-time Army, but Cardwell was opposed bitterly in every move he suggested. The Ordnance authorities, for instance, insisted on going back to the muzzle-loading cannon, giving the Army artillery guns that were twenty years behind those of the rest of the world.

The normal peace-time uniform of the infantry was still the red tunic, but with dark-blue trousers and a spike helmet. The cavalry varied from one regiment to another in their full-dress uniforms, and these changed continually, and were elaborate and decorative. But on active service khaki was being introduced for all regiments, for reasons of camouflage, and the famous red coat was last worn in the Sudan Campaign of 1884-5.

In 1889 war broke out between Britain and the Boer republics of South Africa, a campaign that the War Office thought would be settled with speed and ease. But though few soldiers had realized this, the invention of certain weapons had completely changed the ordinary tactics of war.

The first of these weapons was the breech-loading rifle, now improved by using a clip of cartridges for reloading. The Lee Enfield rifle of the British was accurate up to long ranges, and could be fired at a rate of fifteen rounds a minute. Also, gunpowder was now smokeless, and a rifleman no longer gave away his position by a puff of white smoke. He could reload lying down, and if he hid himself in a trench and stretched a few strands of barbed wire across the front, he could shoot down any number of men advancing against him in the open. When machine-guns were introduced, with their

A soldier of the Royal West Surrey Regiment

high and accurate rate of fire, the tactics of the eighteenth and nineteenth centuries were as out of date as the Long Bow, though generals were slow to realize the transformation that had taken place.

With the help of the Martini rifle, the British Army had fought several successful campaigns since the Crimea : in Egypt, Burma and India. But then the Army had been fighting against native forces, often poorly armed, and the old tactics, combined with the increased fire power of the rifle, had swept away their enemies. At Omdurman, in the Sudan campaign, the huge army of the Mahdi was blasted out of existence by massed rifle fire from the British formed up in mass formation. In tactics this was not very different from the Peninsular or the Crimean battles. No one, apparently, had stopped to think what might happen if the other side possessed modern rifles, and knew how to use them.

Boer mounted infantry

The South African Boers were magnificent shots, and they used Mauser magazine-loading rifles. They understood the value of using cover and ground, and they operated as mounted infantry, moving with great speed over country which they knew thoroughly. The British, still without a properly organized staff, and with soldiers trained as parts of a machine and not as individuals, were helpless against the Boer tactics.

Britain sent out large numbers of reinforcements and her two leading Generals, Roberts and Kitchener. By sheer force of numbers, and by concentrating on one massive advance towards the Boer capital, Roberts knocked out the chief enemy resistance, and it was thought that the war was over. But the Boers split up into small bands, 'Commandos' (a new word in military language), and spasmodic fighting went on for another two years before peace was signed.

Fortunately the lessons were learnt. Soon after the end of the Boer War Lord Haldane went to the War Office, the greatest Secretary of War Britain has had. Unlike Cardwell, he was strongly supported by the leading officers and generals of the Army, and many changes were made. The international situation was menacing, for Europe was split into two sides : Britain, France and Russia on one side ; Germany and Austria on the other. If Britain went to war, then her Army would have to fall in by the side of the French to resist the expected German invasion of France.

So Haldane and his advisers worked with this in mind. They built up an effective General Staff, and an Expeditionary Force of six Infantry Divisions and one Cavalry Division, complete with Artillery, Transport, Engineers, Signallers, and an efficient Medical Service, a highly trained staff, and experienced commanders. Recruitment was still voluntary, and the Army was therefore entirely a professional one. To take the place of the Regulars when they went overseas, Lord Haldane created the Territorial Force and so transformed the volunteers into an effective force for home defence.

Perhaps the most important reforms were in tactics and the training of the men. They were taught to fire their Lee Enfield rifles at the rate of fifteen aimed shots a minute, and were trained to act as individuals, in small units if necessary, as well as in open formations.

The most elaborate arrangements were made in advance to move this Expeditionary Force to its concentration area in France; timetables and trains and ships were all worked out even, it is said, down to the places and times when the men would find a British cup of tea waiting for them on their way.

The Royal Field Artillery

THE WORLD WARS

In August 1914 the First World War broke out, and the Germans invaded France. Mobilization was ordered in Britain, and the regular reservists poured into their depots where everything was ready for them. 1,800 special trains carried them to the ports where the ships were waiting, and to the popular music hall song of 'Tipperary', the British Expeditionary Force (the B.E.F.), tramped up the long cobbled roads of France in the burning heat of a wonderful summer, the most efficient, the best trained and the finest Army that Britain has ever sent away at the beginning of a war.

The French and the Germans considered themselves to be the most scientific soldiers in the world and they dismissed the B.E.F. as a small and unimportant army of amateurs, though why they should have done so remains a mystery. They themselves had fought no major wars since 1870 and, as they proved in the opening battles of 1914, they had little conception of the power of the modern machine-gun and magazine-loading rifle. The French, for instance, hurled themselves at the Germans in all the glory of blue tunics and red trousers, the uniform of the Crimea, and with much the same tactics. They lost 300,000 men in the first two weeks.

The B.E.F. advanced to Mons and dug in on the line of the Mons canal as they had been taught, waiting with the stolid cheerfulness of the British soldier for whatever might come.

On 23rd August a rain of high explosive shells fell on the British trenches. A pause, and then for the first time since the eighteenth century, British soldiers found themselves fighting against Germans. But the British officers watched the German advance with

The battle of Mons

astonishment, as they saw the thickly massed groups plodding across open ground towards the best riflemen in Europe. They had never expected men who considered themselves the most scientific soldiers in the world to use tactics that the British had long abandoned, after the bitter lessons of South Africa.

A wave of rapid rifle fire broke out all along the British line. 'They were in solid square blocks,' said a sergeant, 'and you couldn't help hitting them.' The Germans stopped dead; they reformed and came on again, but met the same mercilessly accurate rifle fire. The British, they reported to their Headquarters, were armed with twenty-eight machine guns to each battalion. The correct figure was two.

But the B.E.F. could not stay in their trenches. On their right the French were falling back, and as their Allies retreated the British were forced to follow suit, especially as there was nothing at all to cover them on their left flank. The Germans, who were shocked by their casualties, did not press these tough, regular soldiers too closely, and so the B.E.F. tramped wearily back again down the French roads. They were exhausted.

The war had come to a standstill now, with a continuous line from the Channel to the Swiss frontier, both sides burrowing into the ground like moles, with complicated trench systems and many miles of barbed wire. No flanking attacks were possible: nothing, so far as the generals could see, but frontal attacks delivered in overwhelming strength of men and guns. So for four years they hurled themselves at each other, won a mile or so of ground, and lost hundreds of thousands of men.

By now Britain had built up a national Army, the largest in her history. The first of the volunteers (for conscription did not come until later) were used in the battle of

The B. E.F. in the trenches

the Somme. After a bombardment that lasted for seven days, the young British volunteers left their trenches and advanced in long lines against the German trenches. But despite their astonishing bravery, they were driven back with the loss of 60,000 on the first day. The attacks went on for several weeks, still without much success, until the total of casualties reached the terrifying figure of 400,000—more than all the men

The battle of the Somme

The call for volunteers

who had fought in the Boer War.

While the summer of 1915 brought about a stalemate in the fighting on the western front, the Russians were suffering the effects of their gallant campaigns in the east. Casualties were enormous and Russia's communications with the West were cut off by the entry of Turkey into the war.

Lawrence of Arabia

Winston Churchill, who was First Lord of the Admiralty at the time, decided to help Russia by opening up a second front in the east by way of the Dardanelles. But because of the discussion and delay, the Turks had about two months' warning of the forthcoming attack. The British troops, supported by Australians and New Zealanders, finally landed at Gallipoli, but the battle was so long drawn-out, and casualties reached such a high figure, that by the end of the year evacuation of the troops was ordered. The heroism of the troops at Gallipoli is beyond all praise, and had the initial planning by those concerned matched up to the determination of the troops, then Churchill's great efforts would undoubtedly have ended in victory.

After a disastrous campaign against the Turks in Mesopotamia, an attack on Gaza, the gateway to Palestine, failed, and General Allenby was sent to restore the low spirits of the Army in the Middle East. The very presence of Allenby inspired energy and determination.

The Turkish position extended from Gaza to Beersheba, a front of about twenty miles, the right flank resting on the sea and the left in the Jordan hills. Allenby's plan was to take Beersheba, overrun the central defences by a flanking attack from the east, and trap the garrison of Gaza by using his cavalry. Allenby was aided by the good work of Lawrence of Arabia and his bands of Arabs, who were carrying out raids on Turkish positions and damaging the local railway lines. Lawrence had an astonishing way with the Arabs and was most successful with his private army in the Allied cause.

Allenby let it be known that his attack would be made on Gaza, but in fact he attacked Beersheba ; the attack was a complete success, and resulted in the routing of the Turks in Palestine. The campaign against Turkey was a turning-point in the war, and the beginning of the end for the Turkish Army.

Meanwhile, the deadlock on the western front had at last been broken by a British invention, the tank. The first ones looked like huge water tanks, and so they were called as an attempt at secrecy. The early models had a speed of two miles an hour, and carried machine-guns or small six-pounders. Their first real battle was at Cambrai in 1917, when 381 of these clumsy monsters rolled out upon the astonished enemy. There had been no bombardment, and the surprise was complete. The tanks flattened out the wire and heaved themselves ponderously over the German trenches, while the exultant infantry followed behind. But though a great gap had been torn in the enemy line, there were not sufficient reserves to exploit the victory and the attack came to a stop.

The pattern of future warfare had been changed, however, just as, earlier, the magazine-loading rifle had brought about a revolution in tactics. In 1918 the Germans asked for an armistice, and the most dreadful war in history ended. Dreadful, because the casualties were nearly thirty million. More than a million men from the British Empire were killed, and another million wounded.

A Mark IV tank in action

For twenty years there was peace. The Army was reduced once more to a peace-time establishment, and conscription was abandoned. As usual, there was little money available for the Army ; recruiting was disappointing, and keeping the overseas garrisons up to strength reduced the strength of the home forces. The Royal Tank Regiment had now been formed, and the old cavalry regiments lost their horses and rode in tanks or armoured cars.

The evacuation from Dunkirk

In the 1930s there was danger again from Germany, and efforts were made to re-equip the Army, but it was too late. For in 1939, as in 1914, the British Army was once more in France in a defensive position alongside their Allies. In May 1940, the Germans invaded Belgium and Holland and this time they made no mistakes. Their Panzer columns of tanks succeeded where Von Kluck's marching men had failed, and the British, the inventors of the tank, were outclassed in the handling of armour. The Army was still a regular, professional force, well trained with the weapons they possessed, but bravery and training are no answer to machines.

The French were broken and sued for peace. The British fell back to the Channel, and were evacuated from Dunkirk. That was a heroic and exciting operation, but as Sir Winston Churchill said, wars are not won by evacuations, and Britain retreated to her island to build up a modern army, based on the regular troops and those of the Territorial Army founded by Haldane.

The troops were equipped slowly with all the complicated and scientific weapons of modern warfare, and eventually they fought their way back against the Germans, the Italians and the Japanese.

In the Middle East, General Alexander was Commander-in-Chief, and the new Commander of the 8th Army in North Africa was General Montgomery. They formed a perfect combination. Preparations were going ahead for the great battle against Field Marshal Rommel who commanded the German-Italian armies. At the end of September 1942 Rommel attacked, but he met more than his match this time in Montgomery, whose army held after three days of bitter fighting ; Rommel's army had to withdraw. The morale of the 8th Army was now very high and there was an air of excitement and

The war in the Middle East

tension as they prepared for the final blow. This came with a big bang on the 23rd October. With a full moon the sky was lit up with the greatest artillery barrage in history ; from a thousand guns, backed up by air bombardment, the attack began ; by November, after a series of attack and counter-attack, the 8th Army had achieved its purpose. Rommel was on the run and Montgomery was after him ; this was a hunt which did not end until after the battles of El Agheila and Mareth, and it resulted in the surrender of a quarter of a million men in Tunisia — 2,000 miles westward. The 8th Army, in its size, its compactness, and fierce pride of identity, was curiously similar to Wellington's Peninsular Army. Unlike the First World War this was a campaign of swift manoeuvre, and casualities were mercifully small.

General Alexander

General Montgomery

At the end of 1943 General Alexander was in command in Italy, and General Montgomery went as Commander-in-Chief under General Eisenhower for the invasion of Europe. In Italy the Army was holding down great numbers of Germans with comparatively small forces and many of the troops were in the line for over six months without relief.

In January 1944 an Allied landing was made at Anzio, and some of the bitterest fighting of the war took place. It was not until May 1944 that a full-scale Allied offensive was possible along the whole front including Anzio, and the Germans were completely routed.

General Wingate and his 'Chindits'

Preparing for 'D-Day'

In the Far East, the position on the Burmese front had improved under the guidance of Admiral Mountbatten as Supreme Commander, and General Wingate's 'Chindits', as they were called, disrupted the communications and harassed the outposts behind the Japanese lines. By this time General Slim had taken over command of the 14th Army, which was fighting in Burma.

As the war in the Far East came to an end, the final stages of the war were fast approaching, and in Britain preparations for the invasion of Europe, the Normandy landing, were almost completed. The Allied forces in the United Kingdom were rapidly increasing; every town and country lane in Southern England was crammed with Allied troops and vehicles, a force of over 2,000,000, with stores and weapons of every kind. It was a most exciting period; the countryside was buzzing with activity, and there was an air of adventure and expectancy about.

Several ingenious ideas were put into practice to aid the landings, such as a mobile harbour built in sections and towed across the Channel, called 'Mulberry', and a flexible pipe-line laid under the sea from England to Normandy to supply petrol for the armies, which was called 'Pluto'.

On 6th June, the great 'D-Day' became a reality, and over 5,000 ships and landing craft set out from their harbours towards Normandy. So much depended upon those young men of the 22nd Independent Parachute Company, the spearhead of the airborne assault, who were landing behind the enemy-held Atlantic wall near Caen. These men were to act as pathfinders for the 6th Airborne Division by marking the dropping- and landing-places with lights and ground flares. It was upon the success of these men that the fate of the division rested. The operation was successful, and it enabled the division to capture its objectives after some very hard and bitter fighting. Soon a front of about fifty miles was opened up.

A further example of the part played by the airborne forces was the battle of Arnhem in Holland, where the gallantry displayed by the 1st Airborne Division stirred the imagination of the whole world.

Street fighting in France

But complete victory over the Germans was not achieved until 1945. Only then did the Second World War come to an end, a war in which every unit of the British Army played a proud and noble part, adding greater fame and glory to the records of its Regiments, Corps and Services, and adding many new battle-honours to the colours. The contribution of the Territorial Army, that wonderful volunteer force, is beyond all praise. As in the First World War, it lived up to its high reputation as an efficient fighting force, and there is no doubt that it is still the finest volunteer force in the world.

During the Second World War, women took their place on active service for the first time in the history of the British Army. In 1938 the Auxiliary Territorial Service had been formed, and both the men and women of the A.T.S. formed gun-teams to defend London against the enemy during the Battle of Britain. The women took their place beside the men of the Anti-Aircraft units of the Royal Artillery, and also served with distinction throughout the world. Many of these volunteers formed the basis of the present Women's Royal Army Corps, which is now an integral part of the Army, with its own regular officers and other ranks, a military band, and a tradition of loyal and faithful service to the Crown, the country, and the Army.

Women on active service

A surface-to-air guided-missile

THE ARMY TODAY

After the war, conscription continued for several years. National Service soldiers took a worthy share in the post-war problems facing the Army. Many of them saw active service in Korea and in the Middle East, besides other trouble-spots elsewhere in the world. These young men did a wonderful job of work for their country and lived up to the highest traditions of the Army.

Now conscription has been discontinued, and once again the Army has returned to its traditional character of an all-regular volunteer force. To meet the needs of this new regular Army, several changes within the existing structure of regiments were necessary, and by amalgamation new regiments were created. This was a step regretted by many, for regimental tradition, based on history and the memories of past glories, has always been the backbone of the British Army. It was hard for such historic regiments to be grouped with each other, but the process was carried out with great care and respect for old traditions.

Royal Marines land from a helicopter

Conditions of warfare are always changing and the infantry now have many new and more efficient weapons for their role, including a semi-automatic rifle. The modern Army has a completely new outlook. Scientific developments have changed its character, although tradition is still very much respected. The Army has an eye for the future of rockets, radar, and nuclear development. The Royal Regiment of Artillery is now equipped with such weapons as the surface-to-surface rockets 'Corporal' and

'Honest John', and the surface-to-air guided-missile 'Thunderbird'. As the equipment for war grows more and more complex, closer links are growing between the Army, the Navy and the Air Force. Whereas in the old days the infantryman had to march almost everywhere, today he is more likely to be taken to his destination by helicopter, parachute, armoured car or tank.

Welcome changes have also taken place in the soldier's uniform. The famous battledress of the last war is being replaced by a combat dress and a parka jacket. For everyday use there is a smart khaki service dress of barathea material, similar in cut to that worn by the officers, and a modern raincoat replaces the old groundsheet. A very smart and comfortable blue patrol uniform is worn on ceremonial occasions.

The Army gives aid in a flood disaster

But today perhaps more important than all this is the Army's primary role: that of keeping the peace. Since the end of the Second World War it has been fully occupied in this very task. Britain's largest contribution to keeping the peace is her force in Western Germany under the North Atlantic Treaty Organization. The presence of British troops, too, in potential trouble-spots is often sufficient to keep the peace; although sometimes, of course, the task is more difficult when the Army finds itself having to intervene between two hostile communities, as in Cyprus a few years ago, when it had to try to restore the peace without taking sides in the quarrel.

At the same time the Army has to be able to deal with a sudden emergency, be it a minor war or rebellion, or to give aid in a national disaster, such as the great floods in the West Country a few years ago.

On the training side, too, methods have been revolutionized to meet the requirements of the new, scientifically controlled Army. There are Army Apprentice Schools and Junior Leader Units, while for the technically-minded there is the new Welbeck College which caters for a two-year sixth form boarding education in preparation for entry to the Royal Military Academy at Sandhurst. Finally, there is the Royal Military College of Science, where the young officer may read for degrees of the University of London in science or engineering.

So that is the British Army, voluntary, professional, highly educated and trained to use the complicated weapons of the twentieth century, housed in barracks which would have seemed palaces to the men of Inkerman and Salamanca, and fed with a care and luxury that the half-starved Crimean soldiers would have regarded with a hopeless envy.

But nothing else has changed, for the character of the British soldier is still the same as his ancestor of Blenheim and Minden, of Dettingen and Quebec, of Balaclava and of El Alemain. There is no other Army with such a glorious history or with such proud traditions to follow.

The Royal Military Academy at Sandhurst

THE ARMY

consists of the following Arms and Services:

ROYAL ARMOURED CORPS

The Life Guards
Royal Horse Guards (The Blues)
*1st The Queen's Dragoon Guards
3rd Carabiniers (Prince of Wales's Dragoon Guards)
4th/7th Royal Dragoon Guards
5th Royal Inniskilling Dragoon Guards
The Royal Dragoons (1st Dragoons)
The Royal Scots Greys (2nd Dragoons)
*The Queen's Own Hussars
*The Queen's Royal Irish Hussars
*9th/12th Royal Lancers (Prince of Wales's)
10th Royal Hussars (Prince of Wales's Own)
11th Hussars (Prince Albert's Own)
13th/18th Royal Hussars (Queen Mary's Own)
14th/20th King's Hussars
15th/19th The King's Royal Hussars
16th/5th The Queen's Royal Lancers
17th/21st Lancers
Royal Tank Regiment

ROYAL REGIMENT OF ARTILLERY (*Incl. Royal Horse Artillery*)

CORPS OF ROYAL ENGINEERS

ROYAL CORPS OF SIGNALS

[redacted]

FOOT GUARDS AND INFANTRY (BY BRIGADES)

Guards
Grenadier Guards
Coldstream Guards
Scots Guards
Irish Guards
Welsh Guards

Lowland
The Royal Scots (The Royal Regiment)
*The Royal Highland Fusiliers (Princess Margaret's Own Glasgow and Ayrshire Regiment)
The King's Own Scottish Borderers
The Cameronians (Scottish Rifles)

Home Counties
*The Queen's Royal Surrey Regiment
*The Queen's Own Buffs, The Royal Kent Regiment
The Royal Sussex Regiment
The Middlesex Regiment (Duke of Cambridge's Own)

Lancastrian
*The King's Own Royal Border Regiment
*The King's Regiment (Manchester and Liverpool)
*The Lancashire Regiment (Prince of Wales's Volunteers)
The Loyal Regiment (North Lancashire)

Fusilier
The Royal Northumberland Fusiliers
‡The Royal Warwickshire Fusiliers
The Royal Fusiliers (City of London Regiment)
The Lancashire Fusiliers

East Anglian
*1st East Anglian Regiment (Royal Norfolk and Suffolk)
*2nd East Anglian Regiment (Duchess of Gloucester's Own Royal Lincolnshire and Northamptonshire)
*3rd East Anglian Regiment (16th/44th Foot)
The Royal Leicestershire Regiment

Wessex
*The Devonshire and Dorset Regiment
The Gloucestershire Regiment
The Royal Hampshire Regiment
*The Duke of Edinburgh's Royal Regiment (Berkshire and Wiltshire)

Light Infantry
*The Somerset and Cornwall Light Infantry
The King's Own Yorkshire Light Infantry
The King's Shropshire Light Infantry
The Durham Light Infantry

Yorkshire	*The Prince of Wales's Own Regiment of Yorkshire The Green Howards (Alexandra, Princess of Wales's Own Yorkshire Regiment) The Duke of Wellington's Regiment (West Riding) The York and Lancaster Regiment
Mercian	The Cheshire Regiment The Worcestershire Regiment *The Staffordshire Regiment (The Prince of Wales's) The Sherwood Foresters (Nottinghamshire and Derbyshire Regiment)
Welsh	The Royal Welch Fusiliers The South Wales Borderers The Welch Regiment
North Irish	The Royal Inniskilling Fusiliers The Royal Ulster Rifles The Royal Irish Fusiliers (Princess Victoria's)
Highland	The Black Watch (Royal Highland Regiment) *Queen's Own Highlanders (Seaforth and Camerons) The Gordon Highlanders The Argyll and Sutherland Highlanders (Princess Louise's)
Green Jackets	†1st Green Jackets, 43rd and 52nd †2nd Green Jackets, The King's Royal Rifle Corps †3rd Green Jackets, The Rifle Brigade
Parachute Regiment	1st Battalion, the Parachute Regiment 2nd Battalion, the Parachute Regiment 3rd Battalion, the Parachute Regiment
The Brigade of Gurkhas	2nd King Edward VII's Own Gurkha Rifles (The Sirmoor Rifles) 6th Queen Elizabeth's Own Gurkha Rifles 7th Duke of Edinburgh's Own Gurkha Rifles 10th Princess Mary's Own Gurkha Rifles

Special Air Service Regiment

Army Air Corps

Royal Malta Artillery

Royal Army Chaplain's Department

Royal Army Service Corps

Royal Army Medical Corps

Royal Army Ordnance Corps

Corps of Royal Electrical and Mechanical Engineers

Corps of Royal Military Police

Royal Army Pay Corps

Royal Army Veterinary Corps

Small Arms Schools Corps

Military Provost Staff Corps

Royal Army Educational Corps

Royal Army Dental Corps

Royal Pioneer Corps

Intelligence Corps

Army Physical Training Corps

Army Catering Corps

Queen Alexandra's Royal Army Nursing Corps

Women's Royal Army Corps

*Formed by amalgamation of regiments, between 1958 and 1961 †Redesignated, 1958 ‡Redesignated, 1963